D1431268

THE NATIONAL POETRY SERIES

The National Poetry Series was established in 1978 to publish five collections of poetry annually through five participating publishers. The manuscripts are selected by five poets of national reputation. Publication is funded by James A. Michener, the Copernicus Society of America, Edward J. Piszek, the Lannan Foundation, the National Endowment for the Arts, and the Tiny Tiger Foundation.

1995 Competition Winners

Heather Allen, *Leaving a Shadow*
Selected by Denise Levertov, published by Copper Canyon Press

Marcus Cafagna, *The Broken World*
Selected by Yusef Komunyakaa, published by the University of Illinois Press

Daniel Hall, *Strange Relation*
Selected by Mark Doty, published by Penguin Books

Juliana Spahr, *Response*
Selected by Lyn Hejinian, published by Sun & Moon Press

Karen Volkman, *Crash's Law*
Selected by Heather McHugh, published by W.W. Norton

PENGUIN BOOKS

STRANGE RELATION

Daniel Hall's first book, *Hermit With Landscape*, was chosen by James Merrill for the Yale Series of Younger Poets. He has been a winner of the "Discovery"/*The Nation* award, and a recipient of grants from the Ingram Merrill Foundation and the National Endowment for the Arts. In 1992–93 he spent a year in Asia as an Amy Lowell Traveling Scholar. He lives in Amherst, Massachusetts.

STRANGE
RELATION

DANIEL HALL

PENGUIN BOOKS

PENGUIN BOOKS

Published by the Penguin Group
Penguin Books USA Inc., 375 Hudson Street,
New York, New York 10014, U.S.A.
Penguin Books Ltd, 27 Wrights Lane,
London W8 5TZ, England
Penguin Books Australia Ltd, Ringwood,
Victoria, Australia
Penguin Books Canada Ltd, 10 Alcorn Avenue,
Toronto, Ontario, Canada M4V 3B2
Penguin Books (N.Z.) Ltd, 182–190 Wairau Road,
Auckland 10, New Zealand

Penguin Books Ltd, Registered Offices:
Harmondsworth, Middlesex, England

First published in Penguin Books 1996

1 3 5 7 9 10 8 6 4 2

LIBRARY OF CONGRESS CATALOGING IN PUBLICATION DATA
Hall, Daniel, 1952–
Strange relation/Daniel Hall.
p. cm.
ISBN 0 14 05.8771 3
I. Title.
PS3558.A3645S77 1996
811'.54—dc20   95–43875

Printed in the United States of America
Set in Stempel Garamond
Designed by Junie Lee

ACKNOWLEDGMENTS

I am very grateful to the Ingram Merrill Foundation and the
National Endowment for the Arts for their support; and to the
Amy Lowell Trust for enabling me to spend a year in Asia,
where much of this book was written. Also, for their generosity
and kindness to me during that year, I wish to thank Fan Ying,
Wang Ruozhen, Xia Boyao, Lau Chin Wah, Pham Thi Ut,
Tadashi and Michiko Ohachi, and Xia Bing.

Grateful acknowledgment is made to the editors of the following
journals, where some of these poems appeared for the first time:
The Emily Dickinson Society of Japan Newsletter: "At the Grave
of Emily Dickinson"; *The New Republic*: "Mangosteens," "Sal-
vage," "Son"; *The Paris Review*: "Bartholomew's Cobble"; *Po-
etry*: "A Fifties 4th," "Winged Torso of Eros"; *The Yale
Review*: "The Beanstalk," "Chez Nguyen," "Rising and
Falling," "A Trellis."

Contents

STRANGE

RELATION

1

THE CHILDREN'S HOUR

I have you fast in my fortress,
And will not let you depart,
But put you down into the dungeon
In the round-tower of my heart.
—Longfellow

A FIFTIES 4TH

Word came down: the show
would go on, in spite of fog
thick as water. Then the initial
stumpf, and a rocket rose

to a dead-center, rib-
rattling concussion, like a fist
of the sea balked in granite
underfoot. But where skies past

had given way to meadows
of mullein and boneset, dandelions
gone to seed, asters distinct
to each separate petal, was

vacancy, erasure, something
on the order of mood or inkling
washed over the cranium
like Adams's ur-memory

of sunlight, warming to scarlet
fever and cooling to an original

apple. . . . And another neuron
fired deep in gray matter. Strange,

that neither one of *us*
paid it any mind: misled,
let down, we writhed and jigged
our rank impatience, tugging

at sleeves that might as well
have been empty, so far gone
was every grown-up heart, so high
on violence stripped of imagery,

resounding to the sternum struck
like a tuning fork—*Yes*
this is what it was or
must have been or will be like—

until the grand finale's
numbing redundancy woke
them out of it—the new TV
already on the fritz, its glow

clicked off. And then the slow
dispersal, car and home. By morning
things might be clearer, resolved
to a high-strung world repeated

in each screen's compound eye,
a myriad blind eyes simplifying,
simplifying. . . . In the meantime,
we slipped under a nightlong spell

of lulling, gut-thrumming tones
too deep to trace the source,
and my mother and father, my brother
and I—we all slept like children.

THE BEANSTALK

for my father

Night shift freed you up for an afternoon
with me. Beyond the shades, the world
dimmed and brightened, but our dusk held:
your chest rising beside me, mountainous,
loud with booming passages, a heartbeat
truer than my own vowing to go on
and on. The boy's troubles would go on and on,
if he couldn't remember between one telling
and the next the worth of things, the treachery
of strangers, or to do what he was told.
Curled against you, eyes drifting upward
and inward, I would struggle to the end
of every story. And if *you* slept, the tale
would continue, embellishments unfurling,
leaflets arranged according to patterns
lost on me yet, up and up, without ending,
without change. Your breathing slowed until
you were snoring a regular thunder; inside me
all of summer clouded over, the trees
lifting and twisting as we ran for shelter
under them. . . . And I was falling, half-afraid
of my love, of waking blinded, forsaken,
with nothing to lead me, hand over hand,
leaf by leaf, back to that dark place.

Son

He sent this key from Florida,
I think. A key to what?
I tried the car, the trucks,
tried every door—nothing fit.
My wife thought it was his idea
of a joke. I never got his jokes.

Not a word from him, just things:
a blank postcard from Colorado Springs;
a snapshot of himself from Aspen,
arm in arm with somebody, but
both faces had been scissored out.
A sign above the bar said SHIT HAPPENS.

Eugene, Spokane. . . . He'd telephone,
collect, and I knew it was him,
though he always used a different name.
At times enough to make you laugh:
Call from Hans, Ricardo, Jeff,
will you accept? Yes. Dial tone.

Yes, shit happens, and we pay
for it. How many years
I've relived our disasters,

over and over, the final scene
distant and tinny, like a TV screen. . . .
I can still feel the sway

of lights, hear the bark
and cough of the trooper's radio.
He looked around, tipped his hat back,
whistled. "Friend, what I would do,
I'd get me a court order, number one.
I'd call a locksmith." My own son.

Look at the blue above those hills:
this country takes my breath away.
I own the land out to those hills
and more, good land, the purest air
south of Canada. When nights are clear
we get Chicago, Baton Rouge, L.A.

Black Squirrels

As if the ordinary grays
had faded from being
seen too often, or too often
overlooked; or as if,
too long in the dyeing, these
had been reborn, and the race
renewed. Only a morph, the biologist
droned as we watched a pair
retrace their double helix
up and down a tree—not
a separate species. Whatever:
it wasn't Nature but one of us
brought them here, an experiment
gone harmlessly haywire
how many years ago when four
escaped. Eight, sixteen, thirty-two . . .
Not so you'd notice, at first:
dispersing, they made themselves
scarce, little astonishments
going off all over town. "I saw
the strangest thing today—"

I saw one yesterday
plastered to the street, its

tail still ticking in the wind,
head craned a little up
and forward, hitting a note
out of my range, a twist
of gore clamped between
perfect yellow teeth. I ran
a fingertip across one paw's
individual knuckles, stroked
the glossy belly, again
and again, until I found myself

lost in the voluptuous dark
of my father's mother's coat.
Once a year, or every other,
it hung in our hall closet,
hung heavy in a nebula
of talcum and rosewater, all
cool caresses and warm depths.
From where I watched, the colors
of the living room (a room
she called the parlor)
gleamed bright as a cartoon.
She was talking, he never
listened, never answered.
Her blue rinse incandesced,
she waved a cigarette, exhaled:
"You know where I'd like to go?"
Nothing. "Singapore." *Singapore,*
I whispered into the satin
against my cheek, fists full
of softness. . . . Then a slow
dissolve: the arctic light

of a hospital; another decade
and another question, one
he can't ignore, I hear him say,
"OK, let's let her go."
                    A ratchety
fuss from a branch above—
or I invented it, then or now,
I can't remember anymore.
If he asks what this is all about,
what can I tell him? Nothing?
His mother's son, he can still add
two and two. I could tell him
I'd seen suspicious traces, diggings
at the corners of the yard,
seen a trail of prints, precise
as fetal hands, stamped
across the driveway's new snow.

FINN

What are you, lost within this timeless spell?
You are your father's father, and the stream—
                    Hart Crane, *"The River"*

He sent me away when I was old enough
to travel—for proper schooling, he told me,
but until news of his illness reached me,
I stayed away. And so a generation passed
them by: the dust still settling on that backwater,
sons of whittlers risen to their stations,
a mockingbird's lunatic rigmarole
unspooling, unchanging. . . . He had changed, though:
half-mad, broken, small as a boy. He smiled,
remembered most of what had happened there,
could still feel it, I think, the initial nudge
of the pole that sent the riverbank spinning
northward. But his stories, how he'd bore me
with the telling, how they built up and shifted,
fluid as silt—"I took a dipper and a tin cup
and my own saw and two blankets, and the skillet
and the coffeepot—" He faltered. The time,
where had it gone? Or had it? Time was, a life
consisted in what a man thought about all day.
A waste of time. Another smile. Oh, he reckoned

things had worked out better than expected—
why let it end badly? He'd been through this
twice already, and this time he wanted to die,
as everyone does, in his sleep. But he died
in his dreams: I leaned back into the dark
and watched him make his way, thrashing and weeping,
through their fogs and clarities, a wildness
rising up in him, all full of tears
and flapdoodle, a lucent bubble-stream
of selves I didn't know, voices to match,
white and colored, old man, little girl—
what was happening? *They're coming but I*
won't go   Oh they're here   don't touch me   don't
hands off! I thought he'd go on forever, spilling
his slopbucket of secrets and remorse
till I was ready to send the old fool to hell
with my own hands, beside myself with shame,
with fury. . . . Too late, I thought to ask: the money,
damn it, where is it, my inheritance?
A whisper from the next room: *Might's well*
throw that question in the river. Daybreak,
he sat up in his bed, crying for gin! gin!
It made me sick: no better than his father.

I stayed on another week with this
and that, papers, the funeral. A mockingbird
drowned out the eulogy, running down
a catalogue of birds and beasts—his world
mapped out entire. My last night there I thought
I'd woken up, had been awakened by
—well, what, it took forever to work out:
the damnedest thing, a queer thin cry: I swear

it wasn't me—something was passing through me,
breathless and unending, like the keening
of an animal, and my heart trilled, high
and light, deliriously fast. Christ,
I'd had enough. It took an hour to pack,
another and I was on a train, where I got
and stayed blind-drunk—a bloodshot rage, a darkness
you could read by—until we reached the gulf.

A Trellis

for my mother

1

Losing the light,
abstractedly searching myself
for money, keys, a book
I mean to take—

I'm at the point
of stepping out when it begins
again: a deep-down twist,
sluggish at first,

awakens node
to node up the spinal column,
each clenched fist opening
out into space-

time, swift in time-
lapse, cups of breath-blue and flesh-pink,
the heart of each a realm
of sun-yellow.

The tendril tip
draws rings in air like a baton,
    the urge corkscrewing up
        and off into

    vacancy. What
happened, asks the face in the frame
    my eyes are staring from. . . .
        How should I know:

    seizure, flashback,
satori; or some part of me
    still not ready to go,
        rooting me there.

2

Finally home
from Boston, and another round
    of tests it's been despair
        to pass and pass

    (symptoms persist,
the cause remains a mystery),
    she opens the windows
        of her kitchen

    to a deep blue
splendor, instreaming, warm, the sun
    running a high-strung wire
        to the zenith—

What time is it?
What day? What season? Count backward
from one hundred. Tell me
your mother's name—

She reaches down
for a cloth, something to clean the
windows with, opens a
cupboard and out

slips a quiver
of green blades, driven through red mesh,
still reeling a little
from the pressure

that never sleeps,
pungent, fiery, urgent enough
to blast house and garden
to kingdom come.

3
I'm sorry, I
forgot to bring a book today.
But we might just as well
read yesterday's

again—or none,
for all you know: "The whole east wing's
gone dark," somebody said
of the not un-

welcome shadow
stealing across the edifice,
        flooding another cell.
            Forget the book.

            Look at this place,
like the cleared scene of a crime, cracked
        glass and headless Hummel,
            cool evidence

        of rages, selves
clawed off like shirts of fire, your howled
        God damn you God damn you
            still echoing. . . .

        A former life?
Then it begins again: a name
        or face, some random rhyme
            unfurls, ascends—

        But by the time
you turn to me, the word has come
        and gone; you blush, then pale,
            stunned by it all.

STRANGE RELATION

Chiang Mai
Christmas, 1992

Dear Joey,
        I write too little, and too much
of that merely shatters off the surface
of everything I've seen and felt—and wanted
to tell you about. I've always left it to you
to sound my depths, and ask you to again.
The distance helps, I guess. Some days I can see
just how far I've come from Massachusetts:
I could go no further without leaving
the planet—as I have no intention of doing,
oh, for years and years. It makes me think,
if not quite globally, in hemispheres.
—And let me apologize for levity
before the fact, but I feel it too strongly
gripping us at our antipodes, Mother
Earth herself: the core of molten iron
almost loud in its magisterial force,
that's always been there, made us, made our species,
and hangs now like a tongueless bell between us—

Some levity, quick! The purest blue
presides after a day of storms (and two
devoured by a gargoyle of a migraine),
an early morning sky rinsed clean and polished
to that never-to-be-forgotten shade, the color
of forgiveness and relief. My coffee cools,
and a few clouds glide across the glass
tabletop with sidereal precision, as if
they intended to go. . . . It's my first Christmas
in a pagan land, and I heartily recommend it
to you, who would appreciate the way
tom kha ghai curdles when the Muzak's whispering,
"In the meadow we can build a snowman. . . ."
(There *is* a cotton snowman in the plaza,
and you could choke, almost, just looking at it.)
Thailand, like Japan, has found the tinsely
vulgarity of Xmas irresistible,
and harmless touches of it glister everywhere.
But face it, anything's better than *last* year,
the hospital room heaped with overcoats,
our month-long vigil, watching her not die,
even bored with her hanging on, while the grief
sank in deeper and deeper. . . .There are times
(this splendid morning, say) when it all comes back
with lacerating clarity—Sweetheart, I'm sorry,
we're just not up to levity today.

I've been holding on to a couple of things
that'll pass the time and fill a page or two.
("They tell stories who cannot tell the truth.")
It's mostly trash, I admit, but what's the point

of having a queer little brother, if not
to get a little trashy now and then?
Anyway. In front of my hotel
is a tidy lawn, some palms, a porte-cochère
thronged with poinsettias, and a boy
in pearl-gray livery dozing by a pillar.
Out back, though, it's a U.S. border town:
a weedy lot crisscrossed with dirt-bike trails,
heaped-up rubbish and a few dead cars
—mise en scène for *the* most entertaining
Dog Town since the pre-leash-law days
of the Fifties. Tireless, alert and (true
to their natures) ever companionable,
they caper and cavort and tussle—I tell you, it's better
than TV. The other day from my balcony
I heard a dreadful yelping, and looked down
upon a couple dancing dos-si-dos,
making the beast with no backside, scuttling
round in a dusty circle, and it *hurt,*
you could feel it. Finally it dawned on them
that if they didn't move, there would be no pain.
So they stopped, faced out like bookends, nothing
between them but a single sorry volume
read and reread, but never understood.
It was charming (in a *very* strange way) to see
them stand so calmly, as if waiting for help
that wouldn't be coming for hours. I wondered
why we say "fuck like animals," when in fact
they look so rational, so businesslike,
so *human* when they're at it. I thought too
of last year's Tar-Baby aftermath

with J, how what should have been brief and urgent
led to months of sticky disengagement;
and there was *your* unfortunate tangle with
[Enough, already: I may be outing you here,
but your linen closet is your own affair.]

All neither here nor there. Here is Chiang Mai,
a city of temples, ringed with hills, a balmy
Paradise to Bangkok's Hell on Earth
(or San Francisco to Los Angeles).
Sunset in the plaza: a warm rose light
at odds with floods of cool mercury vapor
setting a little world aglow—or *two*
worlds, I should say. The one, once so familiar,
took me days to find, or be found by
(four grim months in the People's Republic
and I was lost, had simply forgotten how):
suddenly there was this disco barfly,
miniskirted, coiffed and plucked, looking
me up and down, as if I were a six-foot
éclair. Another light: a ladyboy! I asked,
"Do you speak English, you celestial creature?"
(What is the Thai, I wonder, for Miss Thing?)
She blinked once and said yes. I asked her name,
and she said yes. "And wouldn't you agree
that that player over there, the tallish one—"
I could have talked all night, but she caught on,
blew me a kiss, and sashayed back to work.
The scales fell from my eyes: the boys don't cruise
the bridge these days—it's the plaza that's happening,
in more ways than one. Which brings me to the other

circle, and how the two are counterspun
like coriolus lines: a symmetry
that's endlessly pleasing, and distinctly Thai.

I know you aren't the only choirboy
who follows basketball, but the lot of you
would hardly fill a pew at the Colosseum.
Height queens? You might save a place for me.
At dusk they gather in a ring: six young men,
lips parted slightly, eyes straining overhead
where fifteen feet or so above them hangs
a reticule, like an outsize billiard pouch.
But this game's played entirely with the *feet,*
the point here not the racking up of points
but freedom in confinement, the embrace
of armlessness. There's one in particular
(isn't there always), not the most angelic
of the angelic lot, but the one I'd choose
to guide me out of harm's way, into joy's.
(I'm not alone; everyone's half in love.)
Rules are rules, but each player has his signature
flourish, some breathtaking refinement
of the repertoire, unnecessary but
definitive. My man makes a great hoop
of his arms and lets the ball fall through
(wittily prefiguring his intention)
then, with a deft little Highland kick
he sends it up and out and overhead and
in! And when we roar our adoration
(ladyboys swooning, hands to foreheads),
he receives it by pretending not to—

not to hear, or even to know what he's done:
he paces in a tight little circle, flushed
with triumph, with the rush of perfection,
fleeting, and all the more piercing for that,
all the more perfect. He is golden,
as much a man as lizards are lizards,
he is his own bold embodiment.

As she once was, as you and I—well,
we aren't twenty anymore—but we are thirty
and forty, with thirty or forty more years
(if we're lucky) in the flesh. The decade's
been a grim one, but it isn't all
humiliating farce. You may be too young
to have endured Diana Ross in *Lady*
Sings the Blues, whose laughter played like tears,
and vice versa. Light and dark, pleasure
and pain keep taking off on one another:
I giggle anew remembering the wake;
then an airborne square of gold leaf reduces me
to sobs. You know how the first micro-
second of sugar's message might be
salt? That it's so emphatically *not*
obscures the lesson. But will you listen
to me, who swore he'd never play the Good
Gray Elder Sibling, dispensing bromides
and unsolicited advice—at least
it's never been sensible. The anniversary's
upon us: my plan is to think of her,
then you, then nothing at all. Join me, please.
And then it's New Year's, an event the Thais
—I love this place—observe three times a year.

Will a ball fall in the plaza? Or rise, maybe. . . .
Listen hard for the *ting* of an empty glass.
Old friend and younger brother—sister, too,
you'd say—for the duration, which from here
and now feels like forever,

All my love,

2

BORROWED SCENERY

WINGED TORSO OF EROS

You will never change, your life
suspended here, sealed off from the rush
of traffic and the weather, a twist of flesh
touched and wondered over by the likes
of me. Everything breakable in you
has been broken, but for those of us
who will not see, you take flight with a rustle
of ghost wings—your wings, too,

gone now, snapped off at the base,
even your sex—(a squeak of sole
on tile as Red Shirt leaves the hall)—
Oblivion beckons, you nod *Yes, yes*. . . .
But he's coming back, we all do, to say *No*,
I will never let you go.

A Poem in Portuguese

The first few syllables began
not making sense: not something known
and forgotten, but a tongue
entirely alien, even the roots
so thickly disguised I gave up
listening for them. A boot
slid grit across the parquetry;
somebody cleared his throat. I thought
of children, their small grief
on entering a strange house
where echoes and fragrances dwell
like invalids or matriarchs;
then the child's game of chanting
words until they are abandoned
by their things, page after page
torn from the world, balled up,
consumed in a vastly slowed-down
inward crippling, a ticking
weightlessness. . . . My hands
curled into one another, thumbs
rolling numbly together, print
to print, until it was finished.

AT THE GRAVE OF EMILY DICKINSON

"I wish that I were great
like Mr – Michael Angelo"

Gripping the finials of your severely
palisaded plot, I can't *not* hear
the pop star hiccupping in stereo:
a pair of 4 × 4s are tearing down
Pleasant and Amity, respectively, high
on a single signal. They pick this up
in China, for God's sake, it's everywhere,
and I'm sick of it, and sick about it.
The cars wobble and Doppler out of sync,
drone off like flies. . . . No, don't bother
turning in your grave—allow *us*
to turn you, like something on a spindle:
schoolgirl, agoraphobe, victim, mother
or master, whatever: I'm afraid
that catching glimpses of Eternity
through *your* Coke-bottle spectacles is
hopelessly passé. And when was it not?
you'd wonder, joshing. Forgive me
for asking—but who else can I ask

how a world goes so wrong without falling
to pieces? Emily, lend me your glasses
and your still-delicate ears. Touch
Michelangelo for me. Get me out of here.

COCA-COLA

What I want is a single uncrumpled can,
still factory–bright, held lightly aloft
in the roadside stubble. I want to see the clouds
warp achingly across it, and to hear

the one high hawk's cry drawn out to a wisp,
a flourish perfected over time, that might answer
the crisply branded Circle-R, white on red.

Want it to end with a perceptible shudder
in the wake of an Airstream or an eighteen-wheeler,

the aftermath of something really big.

Panorama of the Rio Grande

Undated. Though exactly when
the camera'd clicked five times across
that particular blip of sun
was immaterial, time there being
(to judge by arroyo and crumbling mesa)
geological. In fact the place was
no more, so she told us, had been
swallowed up in one of El Paso's
periodic expansions. "I don't know, but
the hippies called it holy land." West

to east: in a single frame
the sunstruck hills came tumbling down
to a horizontal, gently curved,
linking the next three like a freeway
through a triptych of western states,
blockish and big, identical
to the casual observer. . . .
The fifth one, though, was fogged
with gold dust, and branded by an airborne
echo of the lens's iris. "Here

to there," she said, stabbing at our map,
" 's maybe seventy, seventy-five mile."

And this place? Miles from even
the defunct highway, how in the world—
"Oh, it don't make no *money*.
Just passes the time." Or freezes it:
the last entry was a month old, or a year
and a month, illegible, like her
perpetual smile. I turned back
to the panorama. Left

to right, the river trailed a finger
of sky-pale light across a world
already darkening. The segments
were lined up flawlessly, except
for the roiling waters— But not quite:
the edges curled, perspective flared,
it couldn't go on forever. I made an offer;
she would not sell. "You fellas come back
and see it again." We guessed
we had better be going. East

to west, the sky prepared itself,
a high warp of vapor trails blurring
and tangling in the jetstream—all this
outside now, from the car, still miles
from the river. I shook the map and laughed,
a little loudly. Up ahead the sun
bulged on the horizon, and farther,
the museum, our kicked-up dust, the road itself
were trembling slightly, sliding down
the throat of the rear-view mirror.

INTERIOR

A leaf falls from the bonsai tree:
ancient instructions trickle through.
There's a man in tears on TV.

The dense, twisted stolidity
tortured each leaf into a jewel,
and jewels fall from the bonsai tree,

spangling the rug. Eventually,
bare bones will mimic "winter," too
(there's a man in tears on TV),

then spring, then summer. . . . But today
they fall as if they'd chosen to,
the leaves falling from the bonsai tree.

The sound is muted, mercifully,
but the camera does what cameras do
with a man in tears. On the TV

the tree says clearly, *I am a tree*;
a strange grief sinks down into you—
Up!
    A leaf falls from the bonsai tree.
There's a man in tears on TV.

36

OUTINGS

1. Swan Lake

My maiden voyage: wide-eyed as Natasha
at the opera, clinging to my disbelief
like a cloak, I floated up the stairs.
Quick gulps of champagne: lights and laughter
bubbled and burst above the noise. The crowd
parted like waters for an elfin fellow
bearing chimes; beneath a chandelier
a grand, tiara'd woman smiled out at me
(or did she?) from her bevy of tuxedos.
But even the novice caught the undercurrent
of a murmured *Makarova, Makarova*
pulsing from balcony to balcony. . . .

The curtain rose. I want to say I awoke
at once, but divertissements allowed
for daydreams, and a multiplicity
of doublings: the Hero flanked by Youth
and Age, dogged by a thrillingly sinister Other;
even harlequin Benno split down the middle—
how could anything penetrate a façade
so overwrought? Act II, Lakeside, I was
already drifting. From the wings, the sorcerer
cast his spell, reeling in Odette (Odile,

her dark twin, still an act away),
even as she signed her hopeless love
to Siegfried. Arms gone underwater-sinuous,
self effaced behind a mask of feeling
no conscious soul would dream of putting on,
she rode into the wings on an impeccable
pas de bourrée, whose diamond tip unwound
the fading echoes of her theme—and she
was gone. The whole world ticked. Then the held breath
broke, nothing like applause: a catastrophic
vox humana thundered to the rafters,
and the opened-throated cries of living men
led me, before the lights went up, to see.

2. Georges Bank

Homebound, our little craft, pitching and coughing,
persevered. We sank back, exhausted but alert,
buffeted by gusts of wind, shut eyes glazed
with afterimages, fragments of an aleatory
choreography, whale and petrel, breach
and wheel. . . . Camaraderie had worn thin,
and we kept to ourselves, alone or in pairs,
the silence broken by outbursts and warnings
("Young man, let's not get carried away!")
—the threshold of astonishment drifting back
so far that when it happened, when the waters
parted, and the dark tonnage was shouldered aside
not ten yards from the boat, we simply turned
with schooled precision, and stared. And there was time
for the little boy to cry, "His tail!" before
the flukes loomed in the air, architectonic,
a submarine colorlessness gashed a vivid
bone–white (though by what none of us could imagine).
And with Time itself taking its time, a mass
grander than the vessel, us, and all our lives
resumed its element with as little swash
as a man might raise.

                      The village hove into sight
at last, its bright tempera façades reworked
in sfumato, from weathervanes to cobblestones.
The boy drifted down through a tolling of bells,
through lighthouse beams scissoring finale
above an underworld of starfish and phosphor,
the surface intact, the deep spell unbroken.

After Reading

How lovely
through the torn paper window
the Milky Way

Issa

Her clean paws tucked in, eyes squinted shut,
Lucy's dozing on Blyth's *Autumn*. No way of knowing
if it ever stops, her little legato motor.
She's been sitting underneath the flowers
long enough for a scurf of pollen to gather
on her yellow haunches. One flicky shiver
and it too will be history. Out there,
through the smeared film of all this—staring, this
not-happening, a tossed handful of bright stars
splinter into color. And the light, no matter
how far it's come, how many years it took,
it's here, look, and it never stops coming.

3

WORLD AND TIME

PNEUMA: 1967

Standing on the lake, I felt my heart
growing heavier, growing old.
He clopped his gloves together,
shot me a look so warm it hurt.
Hell, it's cold! he laughed. *And colder
tomorrow.* Shifting to the other

foot, he shivered an emphatic *God*
—and set revolving into space
another shapeless cloud
of crystals, impalpable, separate. . . .
Breathless tonight I caught it
full in the face.

CORPUS

1. The Lard Sculpture

won't last, is avalanching slowly, like the aged
Brezhnev, like a stupendously deflating
Thanksgiving Day parade balloon. The Old Man
snoozes through the after-dinner encomia,
cherubic, digesting his chicken à la king,
not yet nudged awake for his big farewell
to the Historical Society, and the society's
last round of applause. A pillar of books
is all he'll leave behind, and none too steady,
either, books on books. . . . The minute he's gone,
it'll be toppled. Lard, in this god-awful weather,
what were they thinking? Look at *him*, though,
the Old Man, dreaming of better times, sleeping
the sleep of the holy. And dying in effigy.

2. Shrooms With Theo

The afternoon snow-warm, cool-humid,
a boxed-in, cottony light-headedness

through which our stripped-bare babble
sounds, my high to his high, ridiculous,

ri dic u lous, each syllable a bobber sucked
under waves of gut-clenching hysterics.

Waves of pinpricks over nape and hands:
a pair of doves fucking above us

in the feathery dark of a pine dislodge
little loaves of snow that, falling,

detonate in bright, tightening whorls
of stardurst, sunsheen and snowfleck. . . .

[laughing] You're old enough to be my—Please:
Your're *young* enough, let's say, to be *my*—Sh.

          *

jeans creaking kneeward   still cherishing
the body   outstanding   from a squarish tangle

of rustbrown   his swaying   daylit cock enters
the world   & the world   pinestraw   the silken *fsh*

of skin over smoother skin   the cooling warmth
of open underthings   the world lets go

disintegrates to gusts of pollen   I breathe in
deep   deeper   O quick   spindrift a blizzard

in full sun   Theo   the O—   & dizzily
clutch him   like a stanchion   both hands

to the base   & he staggers   crumples &
comes   coming in   not clots of nacre

but a flung quiver   of needles and pins   hot
or cold   I still can't tell which

3. Ornithology

My father brought it to me
on a snow shovel, its feathers disheveled,
head altogether gone, and said,

What kind of bird was this?
I glanced at the sooty plumage,
the limp fat scaly pink—I'll be damned,

I cried, this pigeon is *banded.*
—Another datum for the lost souls
at the Audubon Society.

The stench grew sweeter. I found
a pair of snips and neatly
amputated. The band rolled off.

My father whispered, Look.
Out of the disconnected foot
and out of the shank, a host

of larvae writhed in milky
plenitude, eating themselves
out of house and home

—and now that we noticed,
were dribbling from the severed throat,
and no doubt filled the bulging breast:

millions of them jostling forth
into the light, ready in days
or hours to rise into the air

and bear the body away.

ASHES

The last few cars are whining down the long dirt drive,
farewell reds blink back at me between the maples. . . .
It hasn't always been this way, the most graceful motion
a sequence discrete to the eye made quick enough,
each second ruffling out into laminations
so thin you might see through them. Long gone, the grand
    sweep
of hands and their cherished, sustaining illusion;
instead, the Geiger's grim chirrup, the digital chorus
of peepers in a darkened theater. Even here: think
of the meadows asleep out past the property line,
still sweet and humid from the sun, flashing for hours
with missed connections—the mind itself a smoked hive,
sluggish and honeyed with long desire, winking out
cell by cell. Think back an hour, that late apparition
of swifts, antic and razor–sharp in the clear cobalt
until someone explained that their comical flight,
the telltale alternation of the wings, is only apparent,
like the stately counter-spin of spokes. Think back
a season, or a sheaf of seasons, when over these hills
a dusky snow began to fall, tracers for all the world
like a fabric unraveling as it fell. But by daybreak
we had our evidence, heaped and swirling, multitudes
beyond anyone's counting, and no two exactly alike.

Rising and Falling

Daybreak, the window stirred
like a TV screen. Late snow,
it wouldn't last, and we dozed on
through its peculiar stillness,
our curves and hollows
answering one another, still.

The night before, after the bar,
a film on video: I turned
from the dark, somnambulist pan
across the snowbound steppes
to see your eyes brimming
with light, heavy and comical.

(You were almost a man
first time you tasted it, high
in the mountains above L.A.
Like nothing you'd known, it hurt
your lips and fingers, turned
your whole hand red, then white.)

It wasn't just the snow,
you told me later, laughing,
but what it made you think of.

Well, sure: who *isn't* half
a thought ahead in all this,
half a thought behind?

Could bear it otherwise?
It is a merciful blindness
that lets us see the falling
as a mesh of wires. Rising,
I sank a hand into your pillow,
cooling, dense with dreams.

CHEZ NGUYEN

A crescent sharpens in the west,
the garden goldens: lawn lush
beneath our feet, callas unfurl
their heavy cream against the snows
of the San Gabriels, and a pair
of mockingbirds spar in midair.

What in the world *I'm* doing here
they're too polite to ask. Each dish
is wafted under my nose first,
and each uproarious joke's retold
in slow but faultless English
amid dwindling laughs. Maybe I'm here

to keep their spirits from rising
too high—I and the absent
patriarch, whose latest correspondence,
hot from the Red Cross, smolders
un-reread on top of the TV:
"Ne faites pas aux autres,"

he grimly begins, then slips
from tongue to tongue in a thousand-
word harangue. The tone is pure

Old Testament, though what he wants
—money or pity or sponsorship—
isn't clear to me, and I wonder

—until somebody steers me back
to lighter matters. Long's mother
offers an outsize, hard-boiled egg
and chuckles between her fingers,
"There's a duckling cooked inside."
I smack it, lift the lid, and there's

a duckling cooked inside, sodden
and spiky. . . . My look's misread. "No,"
she assures me, "the bones and beak
are soft like" [mumbled consultation]
"soft like wax!"—Brain reels
and stomach turns, as I turn

whiter and whiter. . . . Much laughter.
She takes it from me, gulps it down.
Have I failed a crucial test?
But here's another course. The feast
is taking forever, or so they seem
to hope: the only time there's time

for talk. Lam's selling his house
to buy a bigger one; Chau's
out to here with her second boy,
sexed yesterday by ultrasound;
Ho's unit is shipping out for the Gulf
(or not, who knows); and Long premieres

a dance tomorrow night—"For *how* much?
You'd make more money washing cars!
You artists, working for peanuts,
like elephants. . . ." Now they're in tears.
"Peanuts!" Eliot smokes thoughtfully
on Long's T-shirt. "Where's William,"

Chau wonders absently. "I'll see,"
I tell her. Inside, toys are broadcast
as if by cannon, and a million
crayons fan out before the big TV
like a burst cartoon—*Where's William,*
I croon as I close in on him,

sunk down in a chair with the remote.
You can see why they love it. Flip.
Dual air bags. Flip. A purplish
black man, singing. Flip. A camera,
slightly wobbly on its pins, panning
the rubble, the dust-blurred minarets.

January 1991

BARTHOLOMEW'S COBBLE

In theory one is aware that the earth revolves,
but in practice one does not perceive it, the
ground upon which one treads seems not to move,
and one can rest assured. So it is with Time
in one's life.
　　　　Marcel Proust, Within a Budding Grove

Another cow was floating by us,
hilariously calm, bell-deep
in milkweed and tansy. She looked
right through us, until we felt
transparent, the bright blue light
more substantial than the two
shades rocking our canoe. Is it Lethe
or nepenthe eases pain, and which
erases memory?—Another day
of clues and lapses, ramifying
puzzles to be set and solved:
memory, pain. . . . A meander swung us
round under an overhang
of karst, rain-runnelled, grotesque,
a manageable, mini-Guilin
—about the scale, to tell the truth,
China had shrunk back to by then.

What is the *gui,* some kind of
flower, cassia, maybe, "cassia wood."
Like petals, those terraced paddies
we saw from the air; toylike,
the water buffalo. . . . Still no word
from X or Y—surely their visas
must be up? Floating back down
the River Li (no Housatonic,
you muttered), one of us remembered
the date, and the conjunction
of the new moon and Mars
we'd noted in *Celestial Calendar*
before leaving America.
We rushed out to the upper deck
to have it driven home to us
exactly where we were—the pair
a hand apart and moving fast:
twelve hours, twelve thousand miles,
what did they mean? And I asked,
when you asked, What *is* karst,
What's a cobble? Every other answer
either I don't know or
I've forgotten.—A far *clock*
of cowbell. And another. Another.

July 4, 1989

THE VIEW FROM HERE

Pot, bowl and cup are washed and put away.
I've boiled the water against tomorrow's heat:
it's cooling in a beaker by the window. Clouds fill
the dome, a whole system banking and twisting
as a soft wind sips them out: a perpetual
inner weather. The city hisses like a cresting
wave, muffled and remote, as if swathed
in humidity, although we're seeing stars
for the first time in a week. I would not want
to be much happier—if this is happiness
keeping me up, too strong, too lucid, laced
with panic. I think of the poisons dissolving
this city's stonework, how because of them at dusk
the heavens go haywire, a magnificence at the brink
of the cataclysmic, how everything warps
to fit the great blank concavity, flushed
and fired by these man-made hallucinogens:
muscular implosions of acid-green, sulphur,
mercurochrome—colors the Good Lord never intended,

my mother would have said. Whatever news
reaches this far is dire, or worse: currencies
in free-fall, empires disintegrating, jackboots
in Europe and at home. And I sit watching, thinking,

It's so *beautiful,* as if the emphasis alone
might make me believe it, or hide the fact
that it's all going too fast to see, on far too grand
a scale, wheels within wheels accelerating
beyond any human power to— There the tape end
lashes, needles sink to rest, the theme endless,
unfinishable, because as I approach a wall
like certitude, like understanding, my surest instinct
nudges me off course. (You've got the true
Jesuit strain, Buck Mulligan tells Stephen,
only it's injected the wrong way.) I've come this far
not to know, but to see clearly: a whole year
of love, buoying me like seawater, then burning
like brine. A hard death, and another one gathering.

The dome has gone opaque, tear-streaked. City lights
pulse like stars in the turbulence, or come and go
through neighborhoods as the power dims and surges,
the way the nerves will map out the body's contours
in floods of anxiety. Mrs. Hu across the hall,
doll-size, bent nearly horizontal but still hobbling
on bound feet, told me that her son—The Big Man,
she calls him—had an hour to spare, was coming tonight.
Who cares? she shrugged. But the floor has been reeling
with the smell of food, course after course, and all for him.
They'd have finished by now. They're watching TV,
a soccer match, it sounds like. Strange, still not a word
from *him*: he could be imaginary, a comforting
(if unfilial) delusion. But she's talked enough
for both of them, for all of us, and when the crowd
begins to thunder, *Jia you! jia you!* (pour it on, pour it on),
she chants along in her rasping, tremulous voice.

SALVAGE

My little room in the guesthouse faintly reeks
of the nostrum the caretaker left, an ounce
of "Wind Oil Essence." (The name is a mystery,
even to him.) Head clear, I work into the dusk,
the page under my fingertips cooling to gray.

But my mind has been drifting back all day
to the dormitory across from us, close enough
to cut the sky almost in half, vacant now, agape,
nothing inside, I guess, still worth protecting
from the elements. Bare piping of bed frames; dream

on dream, how many years, flown out and up
into galactic dust, each homesick boy a trail
of breath, a moan—dreadful, they tell me, the winters
in Beijing. Late swallows are working the space
between us. . . . When he showed me the garden shed,

who was the humbler—he for its squalor,
or I for the honor of seeing it? Such a deep must,
my vision blurred. Then cleared: under a table,
as bright as stolen goods, my balled-up failures,
smoothed out and stacked against the coming cold.

"BODY AND SOUL"

1

Extruded through the grille,
shaft and oval, this late glory
of dustbeams disperses:

one strikes my face, another,
the attendant's coffee jar of tea.
Wan yellow. Silt of flaked umber.

2

She's droning on about the Three
Buddhas, the Eightfold Path,
the Two Hundred Styles

of the character *shou*; her gaze
drifts here and there, nowhere,
aimless as a mosquito.

3

In the courtyard, a cagèd huamei
sings Yeats's song; notes loud
as cave-drops sound and sound.

Tinny and dim, her radio
conjures a few American tunes.
Unthinking, I begin to hum.

4

One Long set a dance to, one
my mother used to love—one
after another, year after year

recovers itself, revolving
full-blown and balletic:
blossoms in chrysanthemum tea.

5

A foretaste of catastrophe
in the joss stick's lofty carding
of hairline fractures:

the tissue of illusion
itself, slit by a laser tip
hot as a billion stars.

6

Demons grimace hideously,
as if "the cycle of rebirth"
were something they'd eaten;

heads and hands fan out
in pavonian splendor, their couplings
fastidiously curtained.

7

From the armpits up,
the Buddha of the Present
is lost in the depths of the ceiling.

A powerful, lustrous body:
one erect nipple
is aimed like a fingertip

8

over my head, and I'm thrilled
for all the wrong reasons—
"Mired in its brutish

and lustful existence,
the Soul . . ." It goes on
for columns and pages.

9

The attendant is dozing,
the huamei is listening,
the sun, still going down,

at last illuminates
his face. Wherever I move,
the eyes seem not to see me.

10

Outside, a breeze balloons
my shirt, musses my hair; skin
tightens to gooseflesh, ripple

on ripple. . . . High in deep blue,
gods of my own are guiding me back,
half-hard, still dying for it.

MANGOSTEENS

These are the absolute top of the line,
I was telling him, they even surpass
the Jiangsu peach and the McIntosh
for lusciousness and subtlety. . . . (He frowned:
McIntosh. How spelling.) We were eating
our way through another kilogram
of mangosteens, for which we'd both fallen
hard. I'd read that Queen Victoria
(no voluptuary) once offered a reward
for an edible mangosteen: I don't know
how much, or whether it was ever claimed.
(But not enough, I'd guess, and no, I hope.)
Each thick skin yields to a counter-twist,
splits like rotted leather. Inside, snug
as a brain in its cranium, half a dozen
plump white segments, all but dry, part
to the tip of the tongue like lips—they *taste*
like lips, before they're bitten, a saltiness
washed utterly away; crushed, they release
a flood of unfathomable sweetness,
gone in a trice. He lay
near sleep, sunk back against a slope
of heaped-up bedding, stroked slantwise by fingers
of afternoon sun. McIntosh, he said again,

still chewing. I'd also been reading *The Spoils*
of Poynton, so slowly the plot seemed to unfold
in real time. " 'Things' were of course
the sum of the world," James tosses out
in that mock-assertive, contradiction-baffling
way he has, quotation marks gripped like a tweezers
lest he soil his hands on *things,*
as if the only things that mattered
were that homage be paid to English widowhood,
or whether another of his young virgins
would ever marry. (She wouldn't, but she would,
before the novel closed, endure one shattering
embrace, a consummation.) I spent the day
sleepwalking the halls of museums, a vessel
trembling at the lip. Lunch was a packet
of rice cakes and an apple in a garden
famed for its beauty, and deemed beautiful
for what had been taken away. I can still hear it,
still *taste* it, his quick gasp of astonishment
caught in my own mouth. I can feel that house
going up with a shudder, a clockwise funnel
howling to the heavens, while the things of her world
explode or melt or shrivel to ash
in the ecstatic emptying. The old woman set the fire
herself, she must have, she had to. His letter,
tattooed with postmarks, was waiting for me

back at the ryokan, had overtaken me
at last, half in Chinese, half in hard-won
English, purer than I will ever write—

Please don't give up me in tomorrow

The skin was bitter. It stained the tongue.

I want with you more time

Notes

A Fifties 4th

"He first found himself sitting on a yellow kitchen floor in strong sunlight. He was three years old when he took this earliest step in education; a lesson of color. The second followed soon; a lesson of taste. . . . [H]e remembered quite clearly his aunt entering the sick–room bearing in her hand a saucer with a baked apple." —*The Education of Henry Adams*

Finn

"The boy without anything to his name finally has something to carry away. Taking the full inventory of his possessions is a ritual that Huck goes through whenever he is in danger and about to hunt up a new place to 'hide.'" —Alfred Kazin, *An American Procession*

Strange Relation

"If men were as much men as lizards are lizards,/they'd be worth looking at." —D. H. Lawrence, "Lizard"

Borrowed scenery, a term from Japanese landscape architecture, refers to the incorporation of distant, often stupendous, features of the landscape into the design of a garden. A notable example is Iso Garden in Kagoshima, which makes ingenious use of Sak-urajima, the volcano smoldering across the bay.

At the Grave of Emily Dickinson

"Touch Shakespeare for me." —Emily Dickinson, letter to Mabel Loomis Todd, Summer, 1885

Chez Nguyen

"Ne faites pas aux autres" is the first half of the Golden Rule.

"Body and Soul"

The character *shou* (longevity) is a favorite theme in Chinese calligraphy.

The huamei (*Garrulax canorus*) is a popular cage bird in China.

Mangosteens

A ryokan is a traditional Japanese inn.